ADMINISTRATIVE INTERVENTION

A Discipline Handbook for Effective School Administrators

Written by:

Donald D. Black
John C. Downs

Illustrated by:
Tom Oling

SECOND EDITION
(Second Printing)

ISBN # 0-944584-57-8

© Copyright 1993
All rights reserved.

Published and Distributed by:

Sopris West, Inc.
1140 Boston Avenue • Longmont, CO 80501 • (303) 651-2829

Acknowledgments

This book is the result of thousands of interactions with hundreds of students in school programs from Florida to Washington. Without the initiative of the more than five hundred administrators who sought training in the use of Administrative Intervention, there would have been little need to attempt to share these procedures with other school administrators. Their enthusiastic response to the techniques and the resulting behavior change of students motivated us to put in writing the procedures and processes that had, until now, been available only through two-day workshop sessions. We also wish to thank Lonnie and Elaine Phillips, Dean Fixsen, and Mont Wolf for their efforts in designing and developing the Teaching-Family Model from which many of these techniques were adapted for educational settings.

Donald D. Black

John C. Downs

Table of Contents

Preface iii
Introduction 1
What is Administrative Intervention? 3
The Crisis Stage - De-Escalation 7
Obtaining Information from the Teacher 19
Intensive Teaching 27
The Teacher Interaction 41
The Apology 53
Behavior Contracting 67
In-School Suspension 77
Special Cases 85
Rules to Remember in Using Administrative Intervention 89
Bibliography 93

Preface

"Our philosophy of education is . . . " Every school system has a philosophy that is basic and applicable across all levels and all subdivisions. When stated in the most simplistic terms, this belief system usually has few national variations – "to take each student from where he or she is academically, physically, socially/emotionally (and sometimes even spiritually), to the furthest point he or she is capable of attaining." That is a commendable philosophy for a social system specifically designed to prepare young people to be successful, productive adults.

The philosophy contains several commitments for each individual who is thrust, either willingly or unwillingly, into the American educational system. At this time, the methods for attaining the various components of the philosophy become blurred. Can the needs of the individual best be met by a selection process that will place students into select class levels by ability, age, achievement, sex, physical stature, or a variety of other classifications, or can the needs of the individual be met most successfully through heterogeneous grouping?

When the pros and cons of the processes are analyzed, it frequently becomes evident that although the social/emotional category may have been emphasized in the encompassing philosophy, it is often omitted in the implementation phase. Whether the individual becomes a good math student or a poor math student, a good drama student or a poor drama student, a good typing student or a poor typing student is, in all probability, less dependent upon academic and physical characteristics than upon the student's social/emotional skills (Cartledge & Milburn, 1978; Hops & Cobb, 1973; Stephens, 1978; Gresham, 1984).

Social skills can and do have a direct impact on students' success in school. Basically, those who get along well do well. It follows that targeted social skills should be taught to those students who have deficiencies and reinforced when students exhibit proper social behavior.

For elementary students, social skills often become school survival skills–skills that will allow them to remain productive and successful in the school program. For the middle school and secondary students, social skills are not only school survival skills, but are also the skills required for employment–employability skills. Since attending school is the job in which students are presently engaged, they should learn these skills in conjunction with their current employment–school! As contained in the general philosophy, it is the school's responsibility to see that each student learns appropriate social behavior to the highest level of his/her capability.

School is the final opportunity for most of our youth to learn the social skills necessary to obtain employment and, once obtained, to remain employed. The fact is most employers will not take the time to improve an employee's social skills.

Those employees who have social skills deficits, to the point that they cannot get along with their employer and/or fellow employees, are the ones most apt to be terminated. The same holds true for school programs. Most schools do not place priority on the mastery of those social skills that differentiate between success and failure for the student in school, in later employment life, and often in everyday living (Carrol & Elliot, 1984).

Social errors, whether accidental or intentional, are teaching opportunities that should not and must not be ignored. They can be signals that all is not well. The person who has made the error can correct that error if feedback is given regarding the error and if an opportunity to practice the appropriate alternative skill is provided. When inappropriate social behavior is overlooked or ignored by teachers and/or school administrators, the student may later experience failure somewhere in the employment chain, possibly very early. Many students with inappropriate social skills have already lost their first job, the job of attending school and earning a basic education. As a result, for many of these students, success will continue to be elusive.

It isn't difficult for most of us to buy into success based on appropriate social skills. We have all had contact at some point with the really good teacher, except he couldn't get along with the principal or the parents; the really good saleswoman, except she couldn't get along with her boss; the really good student, except he couldn't get along with his peers and teachers. These people are all around us and are in every walk of life–they have the potential to be successful. Unfortunately, they don't get along with people!

Most educators would agree that our basic philosophy is a good one, and that social skills are not only a major component of the philosophy, but also have a tremendous impact on a student's success in school and later in life. And student success is as important in an effective school program as is involvement and coverage (Squires, Huitt & Segars, 1984). Where, then, should the school begin? What should be done to ensure that each student learns the social skills necessary to ensure success?

This book is designed to provide the basis for a teaching/learning process by providing school-age youth the social skills necessary to achieve success in life. The primary facilitators for this process are building administrators. These are the people in education who ultimately see those students with the greatest social deficits–the ones who have been "drilled out" of their classrooms to the "office," the ones who are in danger of having their formal education program terminated.

We're certain you will find, as hundreds of other administrators have found, *Administrative Intervention* probably won't make your life easier, but it will make it better for you and a lot of needy young people!

Introduction

Among the more serious problems facing our schools today is student misbehavior. The general public, parents, teachers, and students have all expressed concern over the issue of school discipline (Gallup, 1987). Even one disruptive student can make classroom instruction virtually impossible (Bauer, 1985). As school administrators, you have designed, implemented, and revised numerous plans to assist teachers in dealing with disruptive students in their classrooms. Recognizing that the seriously disruptive student may be the most difficult situation a teacher can face, it is not unusual that the classroom plans were often, at best, only moderately successful—but there were plans. Those classroom plans usually included the ultimate response of the teacher charged with attempting to resolve the problem of a student out of instructional control—"Go to the Principal's office!" Now it's your turn; what is your plan? What will consistently happen to those students who are referred to you?

The phrase, "to the Principal's office," allows for various descriptive substitutions—dean, assistant principal, counselor, psychologist, etc.—whomever the building principal has designated as his/her representative to assist with discipline problems. **It is recommended that as few personnel as possible be responsible for working with students in an Administrative Intervention program; the fewer the personnel, the greater the potential for consistency.** The actual number of designated personnel may vary from as few as one in a small elementary or secondary program, to as many as five or six in a large school or in a school designed to include a large enrollment of students with behavior problems.

Several reasons exist for wanting the building administrator and/or his/her appointed support staff to deal with students who can no longer remain in the classroom. You believe in fair play and fair treatment—that's a given. You also know that fairness is a relative term and may be viewed in various ways by different people (Squires et al., 1984). It stands to reason, then, that the fewer people who work with students in stressful situations, the greater will be the probability that students will receive consistent treatment and that the variable of fairness can be more easily controlled. Second, there is concern about the welfare of the problem students and others (students and staff) in the immediate vicinity. The intervention process begins by isolating the referred student as much as possible. This will help protect other students and staff from potential physical harm. Third, you must believe that when a teacher sends a student out of the classroom, the student is no longer under instructional control and that the teacher is no longer able to maintain a learning environment in the classroom.

A student is considered out of instructional control when he refuses to follow the teacher's instructions. Teachers, for the most part, are group workers. It is unrealistic to expect them to spend long periods of time working with individual students who are no longer under instructional control if for no other reason than it takes time, and this time can mean less time on task for the entire class (Justiz, 1984). You, the school administrator, should see the referred student to give that student the advantage of a prime learning opportunity. You now have the opportunity to teach him some skills that will become a part of his social skills repertoire for a lifetime (we'll use the masculine gender because approximately 80% of the students who come to you as a result of behavior problems are likely to be boys; however, *the techniques are designed for use with both boys and girls*).

Remember, also, how you got to be an administrator. Most administrators were "cream of the crop" teachers and can still be the best teachers when given an opportunity to help needy students. Before the student leaves your office, he should know

- how to accept criticism,
- how to follow instructions,
- the appropriate posture and voice tone when in a conference with an authority figure,
- how to formulate and deliver an apology, and
- how to accept a penalty, and many other social skills.

Many people will have teaching opportunities with such significance attached to them, but few will recognize the situation as a learning opportunity for the student, and even fewer will take advantage of the opportunity or have the necessary skills to teach appropriate social behavior.

Finally, dealing with students who are out of instructional control is, or should be, a major component of the building administrator's job. If you really believe that the school programs you have implemented are totally for the benefit of your students, you should be using all of your skills to keep these students in the program. Your office should not be the place where students make the decision to leave school—where dropouts are created. Time spent with you should become learning opportunities for students with the greatest need. The way you deal with a student in a stressful situation often determines whether that student remains as a part of your program or leaves and becomes a problem for other segments of society.

What is Administrative Intervention?

Administrative Intervention is an effective method of dealing with discipline problems; but more than that, the process contains many of the elements expected of an instructional leader in an effective school program (Squires et al., 1984). It is an opportunity for the leader to model appropriate behavior, show the student how he can be successful, engage in a consensus-building process with the student regarding appropriate and inappropriate behavior, and provide constant feedback to the student during the intervention.

The process itself is composed of a sequential set of instructional components including procedures for

> **de-escalating disruptive behavior,**
>
> **obtaining and maintaining instructional control,**
>
> **teaching alternative behaviors, and**
>
> **preparing students for classroom re-entry.**

The Crisis Stage - De-Escalation

The Crisis Stage

De-Escalation

Greeting the Student

Any student who comes to your office—whether with a problem behavior, to make a request, or just to visit—should be greeted appropriately. Call the student by his first name and tell him you're glad to have him in your office. "John, I appreciate your coming to the office. Have a seat." The greeting is important. When calling him by his first name, you are letting him know you like him, and by inviting him to sit down, you let him know you are glad that he has reported to your office. Keep in mind, he had many other places he could have been, including in a car or on the streets and out of your sphere of influence. If this had happened, if he had left, he wouldn't have had the opportunity to learn the skills you are about to teach. The greeting will also establish the tone of the meeting—not harsh, but pleasant; not indifferent, but concerned; not punishing, but instructional.

Now that you have him in your office and have given him an appropriate greeting, one of your tasks will be to keep him there until you can teach him the skills he needs. Just because he came in doesn't necessarily mean he intends to stay! So, place yourself between the student and the door. For the present, let's assume that your student is seriously misbehaving and that his behaviors are very irrational—yelling, swearing, pacing, threatening, and sometimes bordering on destructive behavior. But he is remaining and you feel you can still work with him.

Physical Tracking

After placing yourself between the student and the door, try to stay about an arm's length away from him. Keep your hands down by your sides or in back of you; don't point or talk with your hands; in doing so you may inadvertently touch the student or he may run into an outstretched arm and feel that you have attempted to grab him. If the student is up and moving, you will need to physically track him in your office; move parallel to him, always keep yourself between the student and the door. Remember, keep those arms down. There will be exceptions to the arm's length away from the student during physical tracking. One exception is the tracking of the student into a corner of your office. In this instance an arm's length is too close. This may cause the student to feel trapped, and he may respond physically and verbally to a situation which could be avoided. If he moves you aside by pushing you, or by other physical contact, let him go. Continue to track him out of the building by encouraging him to return; if you are not successful, notify the appropriate outside personnel (parents, truant officials, police, etc.).

When you use physical tracking as described, few if any of your students will press the issue to the point of physically leaving your office area. They may walk up very close to you, yell at you and tell you to get out of the way so they can leave, but if you remain between the student and the door with your arms at your sides, tell him you appreciate his coming in so you can help him with his problem, thank him for the eye contact, talk in a calm voice and otherwise reinforce his appropriate behavior, your chances of being physically moved aside or physically abused are very slight.[2]

Verbal Tracking

Most students who come to your office will stay in your office, so in addition to physical tracking, you may also need to track him verbally using a calm, rational voice tone. No matter how irrational the student is or becomes, you must always remain calm and rational. Ask him to have a chair so you can discuss the problem with him. Be specific about which chair you want him to be seated in. "John, please sit down in this chair so we can talk." Use your normal voice tone; don't raise your voice when the student raises his or when he calls you or someone else a rotten name. Don't swear, attack his personality, or in any way threaten the student! Continue your verbal tracking by letting him know exactly what he is doing. "John, you're swearing in a loud voice and you're walking back and forth across the room." This tells him exactly what he is doing and, oddly enough, depending on the level of involvement, he may not be aware of the intensity of his actions or of the actions themselves until you bring them to his attention. Couple the verbal tracking with a specific instruction to discontinue the inappropriate behavior.

>Tracking: "John, you're swearing."
>Specific Instructions–"John, stop swearing."
>
>Tracking: "John, you're pacing back and forth."
>Specific Instructions–"John, I'd appreciate it if you'd stop pacing and sit in this chair."
>
>Tracking: "John, you're talking in a loud voice."
>Specific Instructions–"John, I want you to lower your voice."

There may be several inappropriate behaviors the student is engaging in. Identify them one at a time; let him know what he is doing and give him specific

---

[2] A follow-up survey of approximately 100 school administrators trained in using these techniques revealed no incidents of physical aggression towards the administrators using these Administrative Intervention procedures.

instructions to engage in an alternative appropriate behavior. In addition to using a calm voice, it is important that you identify the inappropriate behavior in non-judgmental terms. "John, you're swearing," is non-judgmental. "John, you've got a bad mouth," or "John, you're acting like a maniac," are very non-specific and judgmental. Within this verbal tracking/specific instruction cycle the student is also exhibiting many appropriate behaviors. Use praise statements to reinforce each of them or each of their approximations. Be certain to specifically reinforce each behavior–not "John, you're doing better," but "John, you're no longer swearing." "John, you've done a nice job of lowering your voice." "You're no longer pacing." "Thank you for eye contact." "You did a nice job of coming down to my office." "Thank you for sitting in the chair," etc.

When we addressed physical tracking and the remote possibility of the student bolting out the door of your office or moving you aside and leaving your office area, we said that you will want to track him out of the building and notify the appropriate outside personnel. You will also want to verbally track the student in an effort to get him to return to your sphere of influence. Examples are, "John, you did a nice job of coming down to my office, but now you're leaving and I want you to come back so we can discuss the problem." "John, if we can talk about the problem, I'm sure we can work out a solution; why don't you come back to the office with me?" "John, I can see that you're upset; if you'll stop now and talk with me, I'm sure we can work it out." That last sentence indicates that you don't have to return to the office; you would be glad to listen to him in the hall, in an adjacent classroom, or some other place that is agreeable. You eventually want to get the student into a physical setting that is conducive to continuing the intervention process, a situation that allows you to leave the student alone while you go talk to his teachers. Again, when you do the process correctly within your office area, the chances of the student leaving are very slight–so slight, that you should never have to track a student into the hall.

During this process the student may engage in a great deal of verbal rhetoric regarding his "rotten teacher who has gotten me in trouble, is picking on me," etc. Using a calm voice tone, you should remind him that he is talking (verbal tracking), and give him the specific instruction to stop talking. "John, I want you to stop talking and listen to me." When he does stop talking, praise him for following your instructions and for listening to you. Do not encourage the student to tell his side of the story during the initial stages of this process. If the student is out of control to the point that he is verbalizing his side of the story, use your verbal tracking skills to tell him he is talking and give him the specific instruction to stop talking. Let him know that you will be going down to talk to his teacher and you'll talk to him about the problem when you return.

When the student shows you he can maintain gross control (that is, he is sitting down in a chair and no longer engaging in irrational verbal behavior) you are ready to enter another phase of the Administrative Intervention process. At this point, ask the student for a verbal commitment to remain in the specified chair in your office while you go talk to his teacher. His commitment must be firm to do this, not "I'll try," or "I think I can." Before you leave the office, the student must have verbalized his commitment to you.

This is a good time for you to take a break. To this point, it has been "hold all calls"; you were not to have been interrupted. Not for any reason! Once you engage in the first phase of Administrative Intervention, and until you get the student under gross control, he receives your total attention! This means not dealing with an angry parent, taking a call from the superintendent, or any other interruption. Until you have the student seated in the chair, calm, with a commitment to stay in that chair in your office, tolerate no interruptions. It generally takes less than ten minutes to get the student under gross control, because it is tremendously energy-consuming for the student to remain out of control. If you use these techniques properly, it allows you to gain gross control rather quickly.

Office Arrangement

The tracking process can be helped or hindered by the physical arrangement of your office. Most offices are arranged with a couple of chairs facing the administrator's desk **(see figures 1 and 3).** When a student enters your office for a sit-down discussion, whether positive or negative, the administrator leaves his desk chair, comes around to the front of the desk, offers the student the chair furthest from the door and, after the student is seated, sits in the chair between the student and the door **(see figures 2 and 4).** Being out from behind your desk and facing the student is not only a practice of good communication skills, but also gives you the opportunity to model appropriate communication behavior where the student can easily observe you.

The two chairs you use for guests in your office should be comfortable, straight-back chairs, preferably without arms. The seat and back should be firm—an overstuffed chair is not acceptable because the student may later have difficulty following the instructions to "sit up straight, feet flat on the floor," etc. An overstuffed chair is also unacceptable for you because you may have difficulty modeling appropriate communication behavior from an over-relaxed position. Your office should be attractive but free from objects that could cause potential harm. Keep the letter openers out of reach, pens and pencils in the drawer, and heavy paper weights in storage. Strange things can happen and are less apt to happen if the opportunities are removed. Removing potentially dangerous objects from sight helps ensure that harmful encounters do not take place.

The Crisis Stage

Process Summary

Be certain to welcome the student into your office; let him know you're glad he came to see you. Place yourself between the student and the door to begin your physical tracking. As soon as you can, ask the student to be seated in a specific chair.

In the event the student does not follow your instructions, continue your physical tracking, staying about an arm's length from the student with your arms down. Begin verbal tracking by telling the student what he is doing, give him specific instructions to discontinue the inappropriate behavior, and give him specific instructions regarding the behavior you want him to engage in. Be certain to reinforce the student for observable appropriate behaviors, approximations, and/or instructions that are followed. The positive reinforcement should be as continual as the verbal tracking coupled with specific directions.

When the student is seated, has stopped talking, and has given you a verbal commitment to remain in a specific chair while you leave the office, you can then prepare to leave the student to discuss his behavior with the referring teacher.

The Crisis Stage Checklist
(De-Escalation)

1. **Student comes to the office**
   a. Call him by name
   b. Thank him for coming
   c. Ask him to come into your office
2. **Get between the student and the door**
3. **Ask him to have a chair**
4. **Physical tracking**
5. **Verbal tracking**
6. **Gross control**
7. **Commitment to stay**
8. **Visit teacher**

The Crisis Stage
Process Review

1. _____ _____ is the process of keeping yourself between the student and the door and moving parallel to him within your office area.

2. When doing physical tracking, it is important to keep your arms _____ _____.

3. _____ _____ is the process of telling the student what inappropriate behavior he is engaging in.

4. When you verbally describe a student's behavior (verbal tracking), you should couple the tracking with _____ _____ to engage in an alternative appropriate behavior.

5. When the student follows your specific instructions and engages in appropriate behavior, you should immediately give _____ _____ for that behavior.

6. What positive reinforcement can be given to a student in your office who is engaging only in inappropriate behaviors? _____ _____.

7. _____ _____ should also be given for appropriate behavior, or approximations of appropriate behavior, that you don't request, such as eye contact, lower voice tone, no pacing, having a seat, etc.

8. After you have gained gross control and the student is seated, you should get a _____ _____ from the student to remain in that chair in your office while you go talk to his teacher.

Answers
1. Physical tracking
2. Down, at your sides or in back of you
3. Verbal tracking
4. Specific instructions
5. Verbal praise
6. Thank him for coming to your office.
7. Verbal praise
8. Verbal commitment

Administrative Office Arrangements

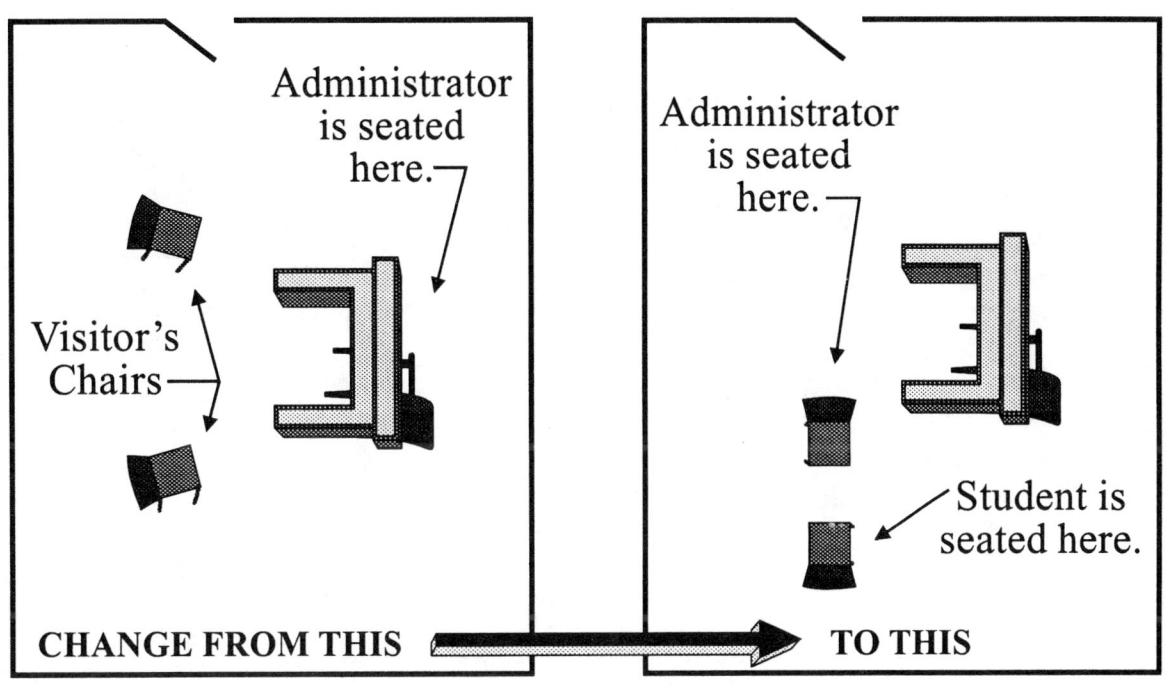

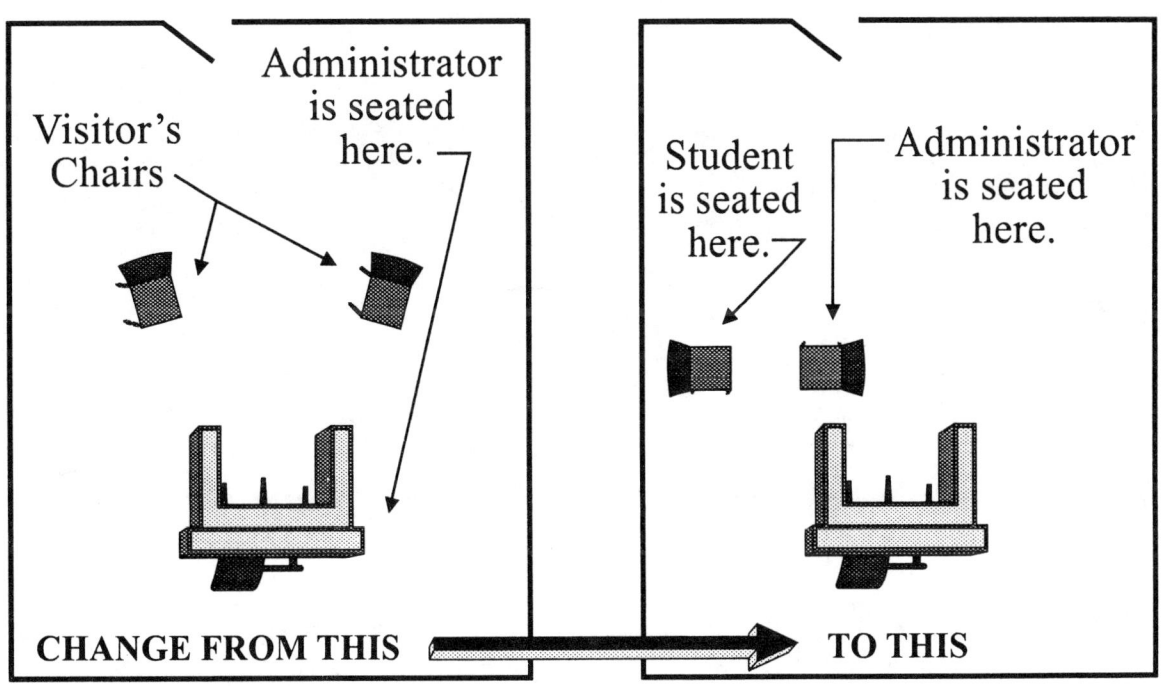

Obtaining Information from the Teacher

Obtaining Information from the Teacher

Leaving the student in your office by himself gives you the opportunity to discuss his behavior with the teacher and find out exactly why he has been referred to your office. Up to this point, the student has received your total attention, but now that gross control has been obtained, you can take the time to attend to other items–the angry parent, the call from the superintendent, the letters to be signed, etc. Before you visit with the teacher, be sure to check your information regarding previous referrals. This break in the action also gives the student the opportunity to further de-escalate his behavior and regain more self-control.

During the process of decelerating the inappropriate behavior to the point of gaining gross control, do not solicit from the student discussion of any behaviors that may or may not have resulted in the student's exclusion from the classroom and his visit to the office. You will be accurately gleaning the real reasons from his teacher. Ask the teacher specifically what behavior or behaviors occurred that led to the exclusion and what behavior or behaviors ultimately resulted in his being sent to you.

The teacher must be specific enough in his/her description to allow you to teach the social skills the student needs to learn. Terms from the teacher such as "bad attitude," "spacy," "a lot of little things," "he just got to me," and other vague statements are of little value and are not acceptable. Take the time to find out exactly what happened. "When I asked him to get a tardy slip, he started to (1) argue with me, then he (2) swore at me, he called me a _____, he (3) rolled his eyes, and (4) went over and stood by the window." This provides you with several behaviors you can describe to the student: not following directions, arguing with the teacher, swearing, and rolling his eyes. Now you have the opportunity to teach the student how to follow directions, accept criticism, and you can teach what can happen when an employee argues with the boss (teacher), swears at the boss, or uses inappropriate facial expressions.

During your conversation with the teacher, you should let the teacher know what potential penalty the student may earn as the result of his behavior. These penalties might include detention, in-school suspension, out-of-school suspension, or in the case of a first or second offender, an incident report or a student contract. You provide the teacher with the possible consequences for informational purposes only. The consequences are not for discussion; the selection of appropriate consequences is your decision. Also, let the teacher know that you will be back to discuss classroom reentry with him/her before the student is presented for readmission. You will not send the student alone, nor will you return with the student prior to your second conversation with the teacher. Remember, your goal is to have the student under control and working in the classroom; the teacher should have the same goal.

This discussion with the teacher regarding the excluded student's behavior in the classroom and his ultimate return to the classroom may be very emotional. You may observe that the teacher is unwilling or unable to discuss reentry. At this point, you should focus exclusively on the behaviors that resulted in exclusion, with the reminder to the teacher that you will return to discuss the reentry process when the student has completed the intervention process in your office. Once you have obtained a behaviorally specific description of the problem, thank the teacher for the information and return to the student.

You are now armed with the information necessary for continuing your interaction with the student; you know specifically the reason(s) he was excluded from the classroom, and you have had the opportunity to search the files for previous incident reports or contracts. In addition, the additional time (usually about 5 to 10 minutes) usually helps the student to gain increased control of his behavior.

Obtaining information from the Teacher

Process Summary

When the student is under gross control, you should get a firm commitment from him that he will remain in a specific chair in your office until you return from discussing the problem with the referring teacher. Prior to your discussion with the teacher be sure to check the student's files for incident reports or contracts.

The information you receive from the teacher must be specific and in behavioral terms. It should be specific enough for you to repeat or demonstrate the behavior to the student. Vague terms such as "he had a bad attitude" are not acceptable.

When talking to the teacher, assure him/her that you will be returning, by yourself, to discuss the student's return to class before the student is brought back to the classroom. Thank the teacher for the information that has been provided and return to the student.

Obtaining Information from the Teacher

Checklist

1. **Check records - progressive consequences**
2. **Teacher describes problem - behavioral terms**
3. **Identify social skill to be taught**
4. **Return to student**

Obtaining Information from the Teacher
Process Review

1. When the student is seated, calm, and you have received a verbal commitment from him to remain in your office, you leave him while you do two things. What are those two things?
   1 _____ 2 _____

2. When you have gained gross control, you are able to leave the student from time-to-time to attend to business matters. **T - F?**

3. You encourage the student to tell you what took place in the classroom so you know his side of the story. **T - F?**

4. If the student is calm enough, you might take him with you while you talk to the teacher to find out what happened. **T - F?**

5. You are to glean from the teacher the specific reason or reasons for the student's being excluded from the classroom. Which of the following are not "specific" reasons?

   _____ He swore at me.

   _____ He wouldn't sit down.

   _____ He lost his cool.

   _____ He argued with me.

   _____ He was crabby.

   _____ He rolled his eyes.

6. You will also ask the teacher what he/she feels would be appropriate consequences. **T - F?**

Answers:
1. Check files for Incident Report and contracts. Discuss the student's reason for being referred with his teacher.
2. True. Once gross control is attained, there can be interruptions.
3. False. Gain gross control (including the instruction to stop talking)—hear it from the teacher first.
4. False. The student always remains in your office.
5. Lost cool
   Crabby
6. False. The administrator will make that decision.

Intensive Teaching

Intensive Teaching

Returning to the Student

After you have obtained information from the teacher regarding the student's behavior and checked the student's files, you are now ready to resume your work with him in the office. You now have all of the information necessary to return to the task of assisting the student in working his way back into the school program.

Upon returning to your office, immediately praise the student for remaining in your office. For instance, you might say, "John, you did a nice job of waiting for me; you're certainly a man of your word; I knew I could count on you." Let him know that you've talked with his teacher, that you have checked his records, and that you are now going to see if you can help him work his way back into the school program. Sit down in a chair across from the student, between the student and the door. However, don't place your chair too close to the student's chair (at least an arm's length) as the student may, at any time, get up and attempt to leave. If you are too close to the student you may not have time to react and again place yourself between the student and the door.

Intensive Teaching

When you have once again set a tone of pleasantness and concern, proceed with the instructional portion of the process. **Let the student know that before you begin talking about why he was sent to the office, you are going to give him some specific instructions that you want him to follow.** Let him know that you feel he is able to follow your instructions, and that you are sure he will be able to follow instructions from his teacher when and if he gets back to the classroom. "John, before we talk about why you were sent to the office, I am going to ask you to follow a few instructions so that I know you will be able to follow instructions from your teacher(s) when and if you get back to your classroom. I would appreciate your listening and not talking. Right now I would like you to sit up in your chair just the way I am sitting." At this point, it is critical that you be an excellent model. You are seated with both feet flat on the floor, hands in lap, and giving good eye contact. You are now going to work with the student on many of those skills you use when communicating with your boss, a teacher, a friend, literally anyone you talk to–good posture, good eye contact, and listening skills.

It is important that the student understands what you are doing or are going to do and why you are doing it. When you begin the Intensive Teaching phase, the student may become irritated and want to start discussing his problem or, as he will often express, his teacher's problem. Give special attention to the rationales for each of the instructions you give. Under no circumstance is the student allowed to overlook any instruction you ask him to follow. **Give the student specific instructions with good rationales and expect the instructions to be followed explicitly.** The instructions you give and the responses you ultimately receive should be similar to the way you would respond if you were to have a meeting with your boss under rather stressful circumstances. You will teach the student how to be at his best when he is receiving feedback from his boss. Tell him you will be giving him some instructions to follow. Tell him that properly following instructions includes eye contact, listening carefully to the instruction, acknowledging the instruction, and doing the task immediately. The student should understand that he is not to talk to you unless you ask him to do so. Be sure to check his understanding of this statement by asking him, "Do you understand?" Instruct him to sit up straight, give you eye contact, place both feet flat on the floor, arms unfolded, hands in his lap, and head squarely on his shoulders, no rolling of the eyes, no sighs, no smiles, no scratching, and no other observable limit-testing behavior. You can be certain that responses won't just flow from him because of his great admiration for you or your position. Often there are many manipulations, much limit-testing, some legitimate errors, some approximations, but, ultimately, success in all areas. Work on one area until you achieve success or until you determine it best to work on something else because you are seemingly getting nowhere. When at first you don't succeed, try, try, again! Be serious while you're giving the instructions about a particular task. However, don't be afraid to laugh with him when he has made an honest error and don't forget to praise the student for successes and/or approximations.

After having (1) provided the rationale for following your instructions, (2) provided the rationale for using the employability skills you are about to teach, and (3) praised the appropriate behavior you observed, the instructions might then proceed as follows:

> John, I want you to sit up straight and to keep looking at me. Good. Your feet are both flat on the floor and you are not talking. That's great. I want you to put your hands on your knees like I have mine. Perfect. You're tapping your foot though, and I don't want you to tap your feet. Just keep them flat on the floor. That's it, you're sitting just like I asked. John, you've done a good job of following my instructions. That's just how I would sit to talk to my boss, except I would probably relax a little. Why don't you put your hands in your lap and you can

> pull your legs back a little, just like I'm doing. You're showing me great communication skills. Now we are ready to talk about what happened in class today that resulted in your being sent to the office.

To proceed to this point in the process, the student must be under excellent instructional control, refraining from talking, frowning, smiling, or in any way engaging in behavior that you would avoid if you had been called to your boss' office to receive some criticism.

Many of the students sent to you will enter your office at the Intensive Teaching level; they are under gross control when they enter your office (i.e., no loud talk, no pacing, and they sit down when asked). When the student enters at the Intensive Teaching level, give him an appropriate greeting, ask him who referred him, get a verbal commitment from the student that he will stay seated while you are gone, excuse yourself to talk with his teacher, check the student's file, and, when you return, thank him for remaining seated and begin the process of addressing any inappropriate communication skills he may be exhibiting (Intensive Teaching). In the event he is not exhibiting any inappropriate communication skills, you want to be certain to take the time to reinforce each appropriate skill that you can observe. Tell him about his good eye contact, his posture, his facial expression, and his willingness to listen. Reinforce all the appropriate behavior you observe and give rationales as to why they are appropriate and should continue.

> Joe, you have done an excellent job of waiting for me and being seated when I returned. I have met with your teacher and we will be discussing your referral in just a bit. Before we do, I want to tell you that you are doing a real good job right now of sitting up straight, looking at me, and not talking. These are all skills that are important to use when you need to discuss a problem, and I'll want you to continue using these skills as we discuss the referral.

Remember, until you have the student under gross control, you are not, for any reason, to leave him by himself. You must stay with him until gross control is achieved. When you begin the Intensive Teaching phase, you may have scheduled and/or unscheduled interruptions. At this point, the student is no longer endangering himself or others and the chances of him leaving are slight. More than likely, by this time the student has seen the error in his ways and may be eager to get out of your office and back into the classroom. Your lack of urgency here can be a negative consequence for the student because it may indicate to him that his chances of returning to the school program are in doubt. **At no time during the entire process should you indicate to the student that he will automatically be accepted back into the school program.** He has been fired from his job, the job of going to school. His boss (the teacher) sent him to see you and until he can square things with his boss, he's off the job.

If he is unwilling to go through every step in the process to gain back his classroom privileges (his job), you should discuss his other options with him, including the option of leaving school. Remember, they are his options. You are providing him the process and the opportunity to return to the classroom. If he won't accept the terms, then he won't be admitted back. If he chooses this alternative, he will have, in essence, fired himself. However, remember your goal is to keep him in the program, not to force him out. The key is "fairness." Be prepared to spend a lot of time giving rationales, discussing options, and teaching skills. An administrator invests an averages of 30 minutes from the time the student enters his office out of instructional control until he is prepared to re-enter his classroom. Some cases may take as long as 2 hours or as little as 20 minutes. You must make the time. Your job doesn't include anything more important than giving students the skills they need to stay in school or on the job. Take the position that you are working with a friend of yours who has made some errors, sometimes some serious errors, and you are not only giving him social skills, but also the opportunity to get his job back, and you don't want to lose him.

The amount of time the complete process may take varies. You are to stay with it until gross control is achieved; however, you can take breaks in the action during the Intensive Teaching situation and during the Teaching Interaction. You may have another crisis to deal with before the one you are dealing with is completed. When this happens, semi-isolate the first student and give the second student your total attention until you get him under gross control. Use your best judgment to decide which one you'll finish first. It won't necessarily be first in, first out.

When a situation arises that necessitates your being taken out of the action once you have achieved gross control, there are alternatives you can employ. You can ask for assistance from a colleague who knows the process and will follow all the prescribed techniques of Administrative Intervention. There are times when it is not only permissible to ask for assistance, but there are occasions when someone else may be able to gain results that, for some reason, have thus far eluded you. You may be very good at the process and still have difficulty with some cases. The two processes that seem to be most susceptible to problems are during the Intensive Teaching and, in the case of older students, during the formulation of the apology, a skill which is covered later in this handbook. Therefore, when you have the student under gross control, and you aren't getting anywhere, it is sometimes useful to let someone else try. However, before you have someone else step in, be sure that person has been briefed on everything that has taken place, such as the reason(s) the student is in your office, where you are in the process, and what remains to be completed before the student can be returned to his classroom, placed in in-school suspension, or whatever consequence the contract or immediate situation requires.

The process does not stop until all the steps of the Administrative Intervention process, have been completed and the student has re-entered the classroom. But you can have assistance and you can have breaks in the action. Breaks in the action should not be interpreted to mean the student is free to attend another class or engage in any activity other than the intervention process. If the hour becomes late and the situation isn't resolved by the time you are ready to go home, you can call the student's parents, explain the situation to them, let them know about the process for classroom re-entry, and release the student from school. However, upon the student's return to school, he must return to your office and complete the process before he will be admitted to the classroom. There are no exceptions; pick up where you left off. He hasn't learned all of the skills yet, including possibly examining the options available to him, preparing for classroom reentry, and delivering an appropriate apology.

When the student can maintain all of the behaviors according to your instructions, you and he are ready to proceed to the Teaching Interaction.

Intensive Teaching

Process Summary

After gross control is attained and specific information is obtained from the teacher regarding the student's inappropriate behavior, greet the student and thank him for remaining seated. You are now ready to begin the Intensive Teaching sequence which is designed to

- **help the student learn the appropriate skills necessary when talking to a boss, and**
- **gain complete instructional control so that you can better teach the social skills this student needs to learn.**

Prior to asking the student to follow all your detailed instructions, provide him with some rationales as to why you are going to give the instructions and why he should follow those instructions. During this process the student should be praised for any appropriate social behaviors and skills he is displaying.

The directions the student is expected to follow include but are not limited to the following:

> refraining from talking without being asked or instructed to do so
> sitting up straight
> good eye contact
> appropriate facial expressions
> hands on knees
> feet flat on floor
> no limit-testing behavior

Having followed all these instructions, the student may relax by moving his feet backward or forward slightly and placing his hands in his lap. He may now describe the inappropriate behavior that got him referred to your office.

The Intensive Teaching section of the Administrative Intervention procedures may go very quickly and smoothly or it may accelerate inappropriate behavior and present additional problems. If problems are encountered and little progress is made, it may be advisable to take a break or to ask for another administrator trained in the Administrative Intervention process to replace you. **However, under no conditions, should you knowingly permit a student to avoid following your instructions and manipulate you into allowing him back into the school program before going through the entire process.** Nor should you become so frustrated or discouraged that your demands and responses force the student out of your school program. Take your time, remain rational, teach and model those skills your students need to learn and use.

Intensive Teaching Checklist

1. Reinforce student for remaining
2. Teach communication skills/instruction following
    a. Give rationales
    b. Give instructions
3. Posture
4. Voice
5. Facial expressions
6. Model behaviors
7. Check for compliance
8. General praise
9. Begin teaching interaction

Intensive Teaching Process Review

1. During the Intensive Teaching sequence the administrator is primarily teaching the skill of _____.

2. Before asking a student to follow all the instructions related to good employability skills, the student should be given a _____ which emphasizes the importance of instruction-following.

3. The rationale(s) for asking the student to follow your instructions is(are) _____
_____
_____

4. If a student does not follow an instruction as directed by the administrator, the administrator should _____.

5. The administrator knows the Intensive Teaching sequence is completed when the student has _____.

6. When you have a student under gross control but you are not "getting anywhere" during the Intensive Teaching sequence, it is permissible to
_____
_____
_____

Answers
1. How to follow instructions
2. Rationale
3. He will know how to follow instructions when he gets back to class and he will know how to communicate with a boss.
4. Give the instruction again or move on to another instruction
5. Followed all instructions you have specified
6. a. Pause for a period of time
   b. Have another trained interventionist work with the student

The Teaching Interaction

The Teaching Interaction

The rest of the process is likely to proceed rapidly since you have now taught the student all the skills he must have at his command for receiving feedback from his boss. He knows about sitting up straight, listening, eye contact, and many other skills. However, before proceeding with the Teaching Interaction, now is an opportune time to let the student know the importance of using appropriate social skills upon entering an office. In the event the student was out of instructional control when he entered your office, your comment might be something to the effect, "I wonder what would have happened to me today if I had behaved in my boss' office the way you behaved in mine?" This point is secondary because inappropriate office behavior is not his primary problem. The reason he was sent to your office is the major problem, and during the Teaching Interaction, you focus only on the inappropriate classroom behavior that resulted in the referral.

The Teaching Interaction is the process by which you teach the appropriate social skills to the student who has just lost his job by demonstrating that he didn't have the skills or chose not to use them. The Teaching Interaction is a 10 step process which ensures that skills are learned and not just taught (Downs, Kutsick, & Black, 1985). These 10 steps include the following:

1. An Expression of Affection - using the student's first name in a pleasant voice tone.

2. Initial Praise - describing a specific positive behavior the student has recently engaged in.

3. Description of Inappropriate Behavior - describing in specific behavioral terms the behavior(s) that resulted in the office referral.

4. Description of Appropriate Behavior - describing in specific behavioral terms the alternative appropriate behavior the student should have engaged in.

5. Rationales - describing for the student reasons why certain behaviors should or should not be engaged in either in school or outside the school setting.

6. Acknowledgment - an indication of understanding on the part of the student. It is usually prompted by asking, "Do you understand what I am saying?" Acknowledgment will generally be confined to comments of "yes," "I understand," or "ok."

7. Practice - rehearsing the appropriate behavior through a role-play situation.

The Teaching Interaction

8. Feedback - specific information about the student's use of the social skills he has just practiced.

9. Consequences - describing both the negative and the positive consequences the student has earned as a result of his behavior.

10. General Praise - a statement recognizing the student's appropriate behavior during the Teaching Interaction, combined with a closing statement.

Take these 10 steps and put them into the context of an office situation with the student who has been referred as a result of inappropriate classroom behavior. Remember, you have completed the Crisis Stage, the visit with the teacher, and the Intensive Teaching sequence. You do not need to give him an expression of affection and initial praise, the first two components of the Teaching Interaction. If you recall, you gave him both of those components when he first came into your office and again when you returned from talking to the teacher, before you began the intensive teaching phase (i.e., "John, I appreciate your coming to my office.") You are now ready to describe the inappropriate (classroom) behavior, describe the appropriate behavior, and go through the remaining components of the Teaching Interaction. In the process of describing the student's inappropriate behavior, focus on the specific behavior that resulted in classroom removal, not the inappropriate behaviors that have occurred in your office!

When describing the inappropriate behavior, you may want to describe the behavior for him or ask him to describe why he was sent to the office. You may need to prompt the student to specifically detail why he is in your office. You know why he's there; you've heard it directly from his teacher, in behavioral terms! He also knows you've heard it from his teacher, but he still may attempt to manipulate the facts and/or shift the responsibility for his inappropriate behavior to his teacher or another person. If the student describes the inappropriate behavior that brought him to your office as "being late for school," let him know that students who are late for school get sent to the attendance office to get a tardy slip; they aren't sent to your office. Ask him to then tell you what he said to the teacher and what his actions were when the teacher directed him to the attendance office. When he tells you he argued with the teacher, swore at the teacher, and didn't follow the teacher's directions, he is describing the reasons for his being referred to your office. In many cases it may be necessary for you to fill in details missed or to describe the entire sequence of behaviors for those students who have difficulty or are reluctant to recall the events.

You can now explore with him alternative behaviors which would have been appropriate. In the case of his being tardy, you would have reminded him that he should have accepted the criticism for being late and, as instructed, gone to the attendance office for a tardy slip. You should give rationales, usually related to employability skills, for the student engaging in the appropriate behavior and ask him (request for acknowledgment) if he understands why the appropriate behaviors are the acceptable behaviors. Once the student understands what the inappropriate behavior was, what the appropriate behavior is, and why he should engage in the appropriate behavior, he is ready to practice the appropriate behavior and receive your feedback on his practice. As closely as possible, the practice should replicate the circumstances that earned him this intervention session with you. Since it won't always be possible to replicate every situation in your office setting, you may have to come up with an alternative, yet realistic, situation that allows the student to display the appropriate skills to be learned.

Prior to the student's practice you must give him specific instructions you want him to follow when he is practicing.

> John, I want you to walk over to the door; we'll pretend you have just come into my classroom and you're late. I'm going to give you some criticism about being late and tell you to go to the attendance office to get a tardy slip. What are you going to do? Good, you're going to listen, and what else? Eye contact, you bet! And then follow my instructions with no arguing. Super! You've got it! That's exactly what you should do when a teacher gives you criticism and instructions to follow! Now, let's practice.

You practice with him until he does exactly what you want him to do. Again, be instructional and be fair. Remember, you're teaching skills to a friend, skills that he can use now and for the rest of his life. Your voice tone is helpful and, as always, free of anger. Following a successful practice be certain to provide specific positive feedback.

A very natural part of life, when a student makes an error and gets caught making it, is the possibility of receiving some consequences or paying a penalty. **The consequences should not be made by you on an impromptu basis.** They should be a part of a well-thought-out plan used in dealing with all students. A trip to your office may, for most students, be consequence enough; therefore, the first time this happens, the only additional consequences most students would have are a telephone call to the parents and the formulation of an Incident Report. An Incident Report is nothing more than a written reminder to yourself which includes who the student was, why he was sent to see you, the person who sent him, and the date he was in your office.

For students who need further instruction and earn a second trip to your office at a future date, a Behavior Contract may be in order. For the really slow responder, the third-timer or, in a separate category, the student whose inappropriate behavior is determined to be of an extreme nature – you might determine this student has earned a more severe consequence. In such cases, In-school or Out-of-school Suspension might be the immediate appropriate penalty.

Even in the event a student receives the consequence of In-School Suspension, it should be understood that the consequence must not be administered until the student is totally under instructional control. The consequence should be administered in the appropriate sequence in the Teaching Interaction.

Positive consequences also occur during the Teaching Interaction process and include praise statements for responding to the practice and for demonstrating an interest in returning to the classroom. At this point it is also important for the student to be told that when you call his parents you will also be letting them know about all of the appropriate things he has done in your office and the skills he has learned (e.g., following instructions, accepting criticism, etc.).

The final component of the Teaching Interaction is general praise. The student is receiving specific positive reinforcement during each step of the Administrative Intervention procedure. You are looking for and reinforcing those behaviors he has been exhibiting that are appropriate. At the end of the Teaching Interaction, you reinforce the student with some general praise; let him know he has gone through a tough situation, he has learned a lot, he is good at using his social skills and good communication skills, and you knew he could do it all along.

Although the Teaching Interaction is designed to be a positive approach to teaching or reviewing social skills, it is critical that it remains a teaching procedure focused on teaching specific skills. There are two cautions: first, **don't allow manipulation and second, don't counsel.** Manipulation on the part of the student is always a possibility and can take a variety of forms. You should be aware of more common forms of manipulation such as: being taken off track to talk about irrelevant points or in becoming engaged in arguments with the student–these are a couple of the more common manipulations. Counseling is a common tendency at this point in the Administrative Intervention sequence because your audience, the student, is giving you good eye contact, listening, and using all the social skills you have been teaching him. However, this is not the time to provide a lecture on appropriate behavior or a listening ear for a student who wants to tell you all his woes. Even though he may wish to talk to someone and talking may be beneficial, now is not the time. However, the student should have the opportunity to counsel with you after he has gotten himself back into the school program and is again functioning in the classroom.

Teaching social skills to students in the office is not unlike teaching academic subjects back in the classroom (Kain, Downs, & Black, 1988.) Certain behaviors or skills components must be present in both situations for the teacher (you or the classroom instructor) to know whether the student really has the skills and can use them. The social skills that will be taught most often by the school administrator when students are referred to the office include, but are not limited to, the following six skills: 1) how to follow instructions, 2) how to accept criticism or a consequence, 3) how to accept "no" for an answer, 4) how to make a request, 5) how to get the teacher's attention, and 6) how to greet someone.

These six skills are subdivided into components to make it possible for you to tell the student exactly what he should do under certain conditions. You can also observe him practicing the skills in your office and give him specific feedback about what steps he did well and what steps he may have forgotten. The six social skills and their components (which you should commit to memory) are as follows:

1. How to Follow Instructions

　　a.　Look at the person

　　b.　Say "OK" or "Yes"

　　c.　Do the task immediately

　　d.　Check back – this component is not necessary under most conditions

2. How to Accept Criticism or a Consequence

　　a.　Look at the person

　　b.　Say "OK"

　　c.　No arguing

3. How to Accept "No" for an Answer

　　a.　Look at the person

　　b.　Say "OK"

　　c.　No arguing, whining, or pouting

　　d.　If you don't understand why, ask calmly for a reason.

　　e.　If you disagree or have a complaint, bring it up later.

4. How to Make a Request

　　a.　Look at the person

　　b.　Use a pleasant voice tone

　　c.　Say "Please"

　　d.　State request specifically

　　e.　Say "Thank you" after the request is granted

5. How to Get the Teacher's Attention

   a. Look at the person

   b. Raise hand

   c. Wait for acknowledgment

   d. After acknowledgment, ask question in a quiet voice tone

6. How to Greet Someone

   <u>A Guest:</u>

   a. Stand up

   b. Look at the person

   c Smile

   d. Use a pleasant voice tone

   e. Verbal greeting and self-introduction

   f. Handshake - this component may not be used under all conditions

   <u>A Person you know:</u>

   a. Look at the person

   b. Smile

   c. Use a pleasant voice tone

   d. Verbal greeting and state their name (e.g., "Good morning, Mr. Smith.")

Many other social skills have been outlined in a similar fashion so that social behavior instruction will be specific, understandable, and consistent from student to student and from session to session (Daly & Daly, 1977; Brown, Black, & Downs, 1984).

Teaching Interaction

Process Summary

In summary, the steps involved in a complete Teaching Interaction proceed in this sequence:

Expression of Affection

Initial Praise

Description of Inappropriate Behavior

Description of Appropriate Behavior (the Social Skills Curriculum)

Rationale

Request for Acknowledgment

Practice

Feedback

Consequences (negative and positive)

General Praise

This is a process for helping students learn those much-needed social skills in a manner that is not only positive but also highly effective!

Teaching Interaction

Expression of affection

Initial praise

Description of inappropriate behavior

Description of appropriate behavior

Rationale

Request acknowledgment

Practice

Feedback

Consequences

General praise

Consequences - Checklist

1. **Call Parents**
2. **Incident Report**
    or
    Contract
    or
    In-School Suspension
3. **Praise**
4. **Prepare Apology**

Teaching Interaction
Process Review

1. All Teaching Interactions begin with the two components of _____.

2. When describing the student's inappropriate behavior, it is important to use _____ and _____ terms.

3. The description of the appropriate behavior will most often be a skill taken from the _____ _____ curriculum.

4. The purpose of a rationale is to _____.

5. The purpose for requesting acknowledgement is to _____.

6. The practice section of the teaching interaction allows the student to _____.

7. Feedback following the practice is positive and _____.

8. The consequences section includes a description of both the _____ and the _____ consequences the student has earned because of his behavior.

9. The Teaching Interaction ends very much like it began. The last component is _____.

10. The Teaching Interaction is designed to be a positive approach to teaching or reviewing _____.

Answers
1. expression of affection and initial praise
2. specific (behavioral) and non-judgmental
3. social skills
4. describe the reason for engaging in appropriate behavior
5. find out if the student understands
6. demonstrate the appropriate behavior
7. specific
8. negative, positive
9. general praise
10. social skills

The Apology

The Apology

Your next step is to prepare the student for classroom re-entry. This process involves having the student formulate the words he needs to say to his teacher to get his job back–the job of going to school, the job of attending classes. The rationales for having to deliver the apology are solid; they are the same as the ones used in real life, life outside of the school setting. The student must realize that he will not get back into class until he can ask permission in an appropriate manner and unless he assures the person in charge that whatever occurred which resulted in his being sent out (fired) will not occur again. These rationales become the basis of the apology.

For some older students, the realization that an appropriate apology must be delivered to the teacher prior to re-entry into the school program can be quite traumatic. The student who has been successful at manipulating adult behavior for a long time and has never or rarely apologized to anyone, may not want to begin now. However, the only way back to the classroom is through the apology. You may hear such things as, "You're the boss, you can get me back in class." This is a good time to remind the student that it was his behavior that got him sent out of the classroom and it will be his behavior that will get him back in! The formulation of the apology, or even broaching the subject, may be a volatile area, and you should be prepared to begin physical and verbal tracking if the student doesn't remain under instructional control. Be certain that you are seated in a chair facing the seated student and that your chair is between the student and the door. When you begin the process of formulating an appropriate apology, you may find yourself back to using the components of the Crisis Stage or Intensive Teaching. If that's the case, so be it! Maybe he hasn't learned all of the skills he needs–not yet!

The student may also attempt to manipulate the situation by requesting placement in another class with another teacher, threatening to drop out of school, threatening to transfer to a different school, threatening to run away from home, or numerous other ways he feels he may evade the apology. If this happens, discuss each option with the student calmly, looking at both the positive and negative aspects of each alternative. Let him know that everyone makes errors and that he cannot spend his life running away from his errors. He must understand that there are occasions when he will have to do what he considers to be unpleasant if he wants to receive credits, grades, graduation, promotion, money, etc. Also, let him know that formulating and delivering an apology is a skill he may need in another setting, a skill you can help him learn. You may not be available every time he must deliver an apology, and you want to help him organize an apology so you will know that he can deliver it when you aren't around to help. Be willing to spend the necessary

The Apology

time to help the student adequately formulate the apology; you are probably the only person from whom he will ever learn these valuable skills.

The student must ultimately understand that he will not return to this class, any other class, or any other part of the school program, until he delivers an apology acceptable to the teacher who excluded him.

The student often wants to know what will happen to him if the teacher won't accept his apology. Let him know that you are certain his teacher will accept the apology if it is done correctly and you will help him do it correctly. In the event he pushes the issue further, let him know that the two of you may be spending a great deal of time together until the apology is correct and that he will be out of the school program and with you until the teacher will accept him back.

Be sure that the apology is in the student's words, not yours! If it is your apology, using your words from his mouth, it may also be considered to be your failure in case it isn't acceptable. You can, and probably will, need to help him put it together, but give him ownership.

Administrator:	"John, what are you going to say to your teacher to get back into the classroom?"
Student:	"I'll tell her I'm sorry."
Administrator:	"That's a good start; tell her you're sorry. What are you sorry about?"
Student:	"I'm sorry I didn't follow her instructions, I argued with her, and I swore at her."
Administrator:	"Excellent, anything else?"
Student:	"No, that's about it."
Administrator:	"I think your teacher is going to want to know what will happen the next time you are given an instruction."
Student:	"I'll tell her that I will look at her, say "OK," and do the task immediately."
Administrator:	"Terrific! There's only one thing left. Don't you think you'd better let her know that you want to get back into class?"

Student:	"Oh, yeah."
Administrator:	"What will you say?"
Student:	"May I come back to class, please?"
Administrator:	"Great! Now, can you put it all together? Begin with your teacher's name."
Student:	"Miss Jones, I'm sorry I didn't follow your directions, and argued with you and swore. Next time you give me an instruction, I'll look at you, say 'o.k.,' and do the task immediately. May I please come back to class?"
Administrator:	"Excellent, just excellent!"

Once the apology is put together it is rehearsed until the student can remember each component without faltering. Be sure to let him know he'll be delivering the apology while standing and in the presence of yourself and his teacher—just the three of you—away from the rest of the students. Since it will be delivered while standing, it should be practiced while standing. Standing also gives you the opportunity to critique his posture. His hands should be in front of him, his feet together maintaining eye contact, and displaying appropriate facial expressions. His personal appearance should be good. Pay close attention to his voice tone, and remind him that he isn't to smile—smiling seems to be a temptation that many students find difficult to avoid. Remind him that this is a serious business. You might say, "You're not back into class yet, and whether or not you make it depends a great deal on how convincing you are to your teacher. You've got to come across to her that you really want to get back in—that you really want your job back."

As mentioned earlier, the subject of the apology can be very volatile with some students. The statement of remorse can often be isolated as being the specific objectionable area. In the event you have worked with a student for some time and you are convinced that he will not say the words "I'm sorry," to the point you become concerned that the student may opt to leave the program if you continue to press the issue, it is appropriate to present the student with another option. This option allows the student to say, "Miss Jones, I understand," rather than "Miss Jones, I'm sorry." The statement now becomes, "Miss Jones, I understand I should have followed your directions. I shouldn't have argued with you, and I shouldn't have sworn at you. It's not going to happen again. May I come back to class?" This is the only latitude that is allowed and it is used only as a last resort.

The Apology

If you are with students who appear that they may become "repeat offenders" (e.g., students identified as having emotional and/or behavioral deficits), you may prefer to have the student state that he **will work hard at** for example, accepting criticism the next time the teacher gives him criticism. This approach replaces such absolute statements as, "This will never happen again." Another option for "repeat offenders" is a statement such as "The next time you give me criticism, I will do my best to look at you, say 'OK,' and not argue." These options avoid the potential problem of having a student make a commitment that they may not be ready to make, and therefore fail again when they break the commitment.

Preparing the Teacher for Student Re-entry into the Classroom

Before you make the trip down the hall with the student to monitor the delivery of the apology, you must return to talk with the teacher one more time. There is much pre-teaching that has to take place with the entire faculty prior to you and/or your support staff engaging in the administrative intervention process. In order to be consistent in their dealing with the student it is important to instruct teachers in how and when to release a student from the classroom. They must also be taught how to receive a student back into the classroom. Let them know exactly what you expect! The process can be presented as part of your faculty meetings or other in-service sessions.

However, you still must return to the classroom teacher and go over the specific process of re-entry before the student comes with you to deliver the apology. Remind the teacher that you'll ask him/her to move to an area where the apology can be delivered in private. You want the teacher to face the student, listen to his apology, and if you, the administrator, indicate to the teacher that the apology is appropriate, the teacher is to welcome the student back to the classroom. Ask the teacher to help you observe the student's behavior and state specifically what he/she can help you observe (the student may "blind side" the administrator and make an obscene gesture to the teacher or clench a fist). If the teacher observes inappropriate behavior that you don't, the teacher must let you know the apology is not acceptable!

The teacher should understand that when the apology is acceptable, he/she should be prepared to welcome the student back into the classroom with a positive comment (e.g., "John, I'm glad to have you back in the class. Let's get started on the work you've missed"). Or, if the class has been dismissed, "John, I'll look forward to having you back in class tomorrow."

Prior to checking with the teacher, let the student know that since he has now rehearsed an acceptable apology, you are going to talk to the teacher to see if the teacher is interested in listening to his apology. Leave the issue of re-entry in doubt. From the time you begin to assist the student in formulating the apology, the student should feel that the final decision for re-entry depends on his ability to convince the teacher that he should be allowed back into the classroom. Obviously, the decision to return the student to the classroom is yours. However, you want the teacher to cooperate and be a part of the decision and you want the student to respect the authority of the teacher in the classroom.

After talking with the teacher, thank the student for remaining during your absence. Indicate to the student that the teacher is willing to listen to his apology. You want him to practice the apology one more time to help him be certain he has it right. He practices again standing up, and together you work on all the components until it's perfect. Now accompany him to his teacher for the final delivery.

This is also a good time to remind the student that you want him to walk right beside you as you go to the teacher's classroom—he is not to walk in front of you or behind you. Even at this point some students may still try to manipulate your behavior or respond to peer pressure by showing their peers or themselves that they really aren't with you and don't want to be seen with you. If a student won't follow this instruction, he may need more time with you to learn the skill of how to follow instructions. This student is not yet ready to return to the classroom.

Under no circumstances is the student to go to the teacher by himself to deliver the apology. Since you are the one to make the reentry decision, you obviously must be with the student. Upon arriving at the classroom and asking the teacher to step into the hall, begin the conversation with a statement similar to, "Mr. Smith, John has something he would like to say to you."

Your credibility with your staff regarding your treatment and expectations of student behavior is frequently judged by your tolerances in accepting or rejecting a student's apology. You have practiced the apology a minimum of three times. With your critique the apology should be letter perfect. You have reminded the student that his return to his classroom is dependent upon his behavior. Don't let the student manipulate you. If the practice was perfect, as you expect it to be, the actual delivery should be perfect also. Any inappropriate posture, facial expressions, voice tone, or missing components will result in termination of the process. Say to the teacher, "Excuse me, Mr. Smith, John and I need to spend some more time together. He isn't ready to come back to your class just yet." Stick with this statement when it is made. John might respond by, "Oh, I can get it right, I'll just do it again." No go! Take him back to your office and help him get it right. Keep your tolerances low. Position yourself where you can closely observe the student, and listen carefully to what he is saying and how he is saying it.

The Apology

The procedure to be followed by the teacher in accepting a student back into the classroom is extremely important. An uninformed teacher with a couple of badly placed words can undo something that may have taken you an hour to put together. Comments such as, "That's a nice apology, but it doesn't sound sincere," or "That's fine for now, but you ought to apologize for what you did yesterday, too," have no place here. However, if the teacher rejects an apology (either purposefully or inadvertently) that you would have approved, inform the student the apology is not acceptable and the two of you will be returning to the office for additional work. If the teacher has erred, never let the student know it. It is important that you give total support to your teacher. Do not spend any time with the student in front of the teacher discussing the apology. Thank the teacher for considering the apology and return with the student to your office.

When you and the student return to the office after a teacher has rejected his apology, get a commitment from him to remain in your office while you attend to some business. Return to the teacher and ask him/her if he/she saw anything you might have missed. If the teacher describes the clenched fist, an obscene gesture or other gestures, you again have a specific alternative behavior you can teach. However, if the teacher responds that "the student didn't sound sincere," or gives some other inappropriate reason for rejecting the apology, you will want to make an appointment with the teacher at his/her earliest convenience so you can more specifically instruct the teacher in the classroom re-entry process.

When you return to the student, again thank him for remaining during your absence. Let him know why the apology has been rejected and that you will work with him until the apology is acceptable. "Miss Jones told me your apology didn't sound sincere. We're going to work on your voice tone and facial expression before you deliver the apology again." For whatever reason the apology was rejected, either by you or the teacher, develop or refine an acceptable apology.

In the event you need to further instruct the teacher regarding his/her role in the re-entry process, the student remains under your supervision. He is not sent to another class or activity. Since he is under instructional control, you may opt to place him in your outer office with some educational materials, a book, some magazines, his homework, etc., while you continue your work routine.

When you have again prepared the teacher for the re-entry process, you must again practice the apology with the student, critiquing not only the verbal apology, but also the physical delivery until the student is again ready to accompany you to meet with the teacher.

The apology is delivered, you have approved it, the student has re-entered the educational program, and he has probably assimilated some of the most valuable social skills he will ever need. He's learned how to respond to his teacher, how to work with you, how to take criticism, how to sit, how to stand, how to give eye contact, how to use a pleasant voice tone, how to follow instructions, how to formulate and deliver an apology. These are life skills, employability skills, and survival skills. Think of the number of adults you know who have had difficulties because they have never mastered these skills! You have been given a golden opportunity, an opportunity to give something of tremendous value! You also have opportunity to build some of the best relationships possible between a student and adult. You will find when you do the process and do it correctly, that rather than severing relationships you will build strong, lasting relationships. Your friend, the student, now knows for sure he is your friend, that you like him, and that you care enough to help him with his problems and give him skills that he hasn't received from anyone else.

The Apology

Process Summary

The process of classroom re-entry, or preparing the student to deliver an appropriate apology, begins after all consequences have been administered. The apology must be delivered prior to the student being allowed to re-enter the classroom of the teacher who sent him out and/or prior to entering any part of the school program.

The apology is delivered in the student's own words and must contain four specific parts: 1) the teacher's name, 2) a statement of remorse, including specifically what the student is sorry about; 3) a statement letting the teacher know it won't happen again; and 4) a request by the student to come back to the teacher's class.

Rehearse the apology with the student a minimum of three times—once sitting down, once standing up, and again standing up after you have returned to your office, having prepared the teacher to accept the apology.

Let the teacher know you are the one who accepts or rejects an apology, but you need to enlist the teacher's help as an expert observer. In the event the teacher rejects the apology, the student is returned to your office and you go back to the teacher to find out why the student was not accepted back into the classroom.

When the teacher accepts the student back into the program, the student should feel welcome and the teacher's statements must be positive.

Apology Checklist

1. Student's own words
2. Four components
   a) Teacher's name
   b) Statement of remorse and description of behavior
   c) Assurance that the behavior won't be repeated
   d) Request to be readmitted to class
3. Practice the apology (sitting)
4. Practice the apology (standing)
5. Prepare the teacher to accept the apology
6. Practice the apology (standing)
7. Deliver the apology
8. Accept/Reject the apology

The Apology
Process Review

1. What are the four main parts of an apology? _____
   _____
   _____

2. At a minimum, how many times will the student practice delivering the apology? _____

3. If the apology is a good one, you might take the student with you to deliver it without first checking with the teacher. **T - F?**

4. When you prepare the teacher to accept the apology, let the teacher know that you, the administrator, are the final judge of the appropriateness of the apology. **T - F?**

6. Which of the following are good reasons for you to reject a student's apology?

   a. Hands in pockets.

   b. Smile during apology.

   c. Lack of eye contact with the teacher.

   d. Not standing evenly on both feet.

   e. Leaving out a component.

   f. Lack of sincerity.

7. If the student says he'll run away rather than apologize to his teacher, you should discuss this option with him. **T - F?**

8. The position of the chairs, yours and the student's, are less critical at this point so you can relax a bit. **T - F?**

Answers
1. 1) Teacher's name; 2) Statement of remorse, including specifically what the inappropriate behavior(s) was (were); 3) Statement that the behavior won't happen again; and 4) Request to get back into the class.
2. Three.
3. False. Always prepare the teacher to accept the apology.
4. False. You must always accompany the student. You are the one who judges the appropriateness of the apology.
5. True. The administrator makes the final decision.
6. A through E. Lack of sincerity is not specific and alone is not a good reason.
7. True. Discuss each option with the student.
8. False. The apology is a very volatile point. Position yourself and your chairs to prepare for a return to the crisis stage.

Behavior Contracting

Behavior Contracting

When students are sent to the office they should be aware of the rules that govern them. As an administrator, you are aware that whatever takes place in your office often becomes common knowledge throughout the school. It has been stressed earlier that you always separate the behavior from the student. Through your actions, you let each student know that you really like him; he is in your office because of inappropriate behavior and you will deal with that behavior. The word soon gets around that you have low tolerances, you administer like consequences for like behaviors, and as a result you are seen as fair–a person who can be trusted!

Basically, consequences are administered in the following sequence: 1) Incident Report, 2) Behavior Contract, and 3) In-School Suspension. There are exceptions to the sequence, depending on the precipitating behavior. First, let's take a look at the sequence in its logical form.

Incident Report

The first time a student is sent to your office during the school year, you administer three basic consequences: 1) the Administrative Intervention process itself, concluding with an appropriate apology, is considered a consequence; 2) a telephone call to the parents letting them know what behavior resulted in their child being referred to your office and also letting them know how well their child has worked out the problem with you; and 3) the Incident Report. The Incident Report is completed in the presence of the student and with the student's understanding–not approval, but understanding. Let the student know that this report will be placed in your file and will serve as a reminder that he was sent to the office on a certain date, by a specific teacher, the reason for the referral, and possible future consequences. **A typical Incident Report reads as follows.**

Date: November 10, 1984
To: File

John Smith was sent to the office today by Miss Brown because he did not accept Miss Brown's criticism. John argued with Miss Brown and swore at her.

John understands that if he is sent to the office because of a school problem during the remainder of this year, consideration will be given to entering into a behavior contract as the minimum consequence.

_____   _____
John Smith, Student   Donald D. Black, Principal

The Incident Report is then placed in the appropriate file. Carbon copies are not sent to other personnel; the Incident Report is basically a reminder to the administrator of his/her involvement with John Smith. The next time John Smith is referred to your office, achieve gross control and receive a commitment from the student to remain in the designated chair in your office while you talk to his teachers. You will again take this opportunity to check the file for any active incident reports or contracts that may influence the administration of consequences.

The Incident Report is generally hand written. However, in order to save time, some administrators prefer to use a preprinted form to write up the incident.

Incident Report

Date:

To: File

_____ was sent to the office today for the following behavior:
(student's name)

If I am sent to the office again for this or similar behavior during this school year, consideration will be given to entering into a behavior contract as a minimum consequence.

_____   _____
         Administrator   Student

Contract

To continue the example, John is sent to your office again during the same school year as the result of other inappropriate behavior. You welcome him and reinforce him for coming to your office. He is under gross control and, as always, you obtain assurance from him that he will remain in a specific chair in your office while you obtain the necessary information from the referring teacher. During your absence from the office to discuss John's behavior with his teacher, check your file for active contracts or incident reports. Your check reveals an active incident report, which indicates that the next consequence in the sequence should be a behavior contract. Under some circumstances you may determine the inappropriate behavior indicates the necessity of going directly to in-school suspension, out-of-school suspension, or possibly an alternative placement.

Caution should be used in accelerating to more restrictive consequences unless the behavior warrants such acceleration. Your concern is for the student and the learning process. You may come under pressure from some staff members to administer consequences that are more severe than necessary. Don't get the reputation of being the person who wants to appease staff members more than you want to administer fair, appropriate consequences.

This time when you get John to the consequence portion of the Teaching Interaction, you will include a behavior contract as an additional consequence. The contract will be in addition to the phone call to the parents and the necessity for the student to interact with you in the office. John was aware that the next consequence in the sequence would be a contract because it was included in the wording of his active incident report.

The behavior contract is formulated in the same manner as the incident report. Read each statement aloud to John as you write it. Continue to ask John if he understands the contents and ask if he has any questions. John may not agree with all of the components of the contract but he certainly should understand them and, if you are being fair, he should agree with most of them.

The behavior contract has six major components: 1) the name of the student, 2) a brief description of the behavior(s) that led to the contract, 3) the name of the referring teacher, 4) the consequences that are administered in the event the contract is broken, 5) the date the contract expires, and 6) the signature of the student and administrator entering into the contract.

An example of a typical contract is on the following page.

Contract

Date: November 22, 1984

John Smith was sent to my office today because he would not follow Mr. Jones' directions and swore at Mr. Jones. John has an active incident report on file from a previous behavior problem.

John understands that in the event he is referred to the office for inappropriate behavior during the time this contract is in effect, he will be placed in in-school suspension for no longer than 1 day, as a minimum consequence.

If John is not referred to the office between now and Christmas vacation, this contract will be void.

_____
    Student

_____
    Administrator

cc:

    John Smith
    Parents
    John's Teachers
    File

As with the Incident Report, the contract is now placed in the appropriate file. In the event two or more building administrators are using the Administrative Intervention techniques, a central filing system, maintained by a secretary, is helpful. It is not necessary that students see the same administrator each time they are referred to the office, but it is essential that the administrators know the behavioral record of the referred student. This is not to imply that the administrators remind the student of behaviors that occurred 2 years ago or even last semester. References are to be made only to active contracts or incident reports. Remember, you are working only with the behavior that resulted in exclusion from the classroom (the Teaching Interaction) and the relevant social skills (Intensive Teaching) taught in your office. The fact that John Smith was referred to the office years ago is not relevant–interesting maybe, but not relevant.

You may have students who have been sent to your office several times but, if there is a time lapse to the point that the contract has become void, that particular student, in the normal penalty process, begins again with a new contract. Remember, your goal is for the student to succeed in the classroom. The time lapse between inappropriate behaviors should be viewed as progress, which does not warrant additional or progressive penalties.

Copies of the completed contract are sent to the student's parents and his teacher(s). One contract is maintained in your file, and one is given to the student. The Incident Report and the contract closely adhere to the guidelines of due process. Some administrators prefer to include the parents' signature on the contract. This is an excellent practice but not always practical, considering parental availability and case load. As a part of the consequence, the parents are always contacted. In the event the parents are not available for signature or their signature is not required, the contract is read to the parents over the phone. Don't forget to let them know how well their child ultimately did in your office, stressing that the problem has been resolved at school and you are not recommending additional consequences at home. If you find parents sensitive to the notion of their child signing a "contract" you may prefer to describe the document as a "behavior change plan."

The behavior contract with John states the minimum consequence to be in-school suspension. However, there are consequences that may be substituted for in-school suspension, such as detention after school, reduction to a lower system (for those schools or programs using a token economy), and others depending on your preference and school policy. In-school suspension, correctly used, is considered a very effective penalty for most students.

Behavior Contracting

Process Summary

The progression of consequences, other than the phone call to the parents and the process itself, moves from the incident report to the contract and then to carrying out the provisions of the contract.

The Incident Report is basically a record for the administration 1) the name of the student referred to your office, 2) the name of the teacher making the referral, 3) the reason for the referral, 4) the potential consequences in the event of another referral, and 5) the student's signature. The Incident Report goes no further than your office. Copies are not shared with parents or staff members other than additional administrative interventionists.

Behavior contracting is usually the result of an office referral for an inappropriate behavior during the term of an active incident report. The contract replaces the incident report as a consequence. However, it is still necessary for the student to go through the Administrative Intervention process and for you to call the parents each time a student is referred to your office.

The behavior contract has six major components: 1) the student's name, 2) the teacher's name, 3) the inappropriate behavior, 4) the potential consequences in the event the contract is broken, 5) the date the contract becomes void, and 6) signatures of the student and the administrator.

The student should understand the contract. His signature does not necessarily represent compliance; it represents understanding. The contract, unless broken, is void in approximately 30 days. Copies of the contract are sent to the parents, to the referring teacher, and to the student's file. Most contracts use in-school suspension as a consequence but frequent contract violations may lead to a contract that includes out-of-school suspension or an alternative school placement.

Behavior Contracting Process Review

1. As a minimum additional consequence, the first time a student is referred to the office there is an Incident Report placed in the administrative file. What are the two basic consequences that are always administered for any negative referral?

2. The Incident Report includes the student involved, the teacher, the behavior, the date, and the student's signature. What are two additional pieces of information included in the Incident Report?

3. At what point in the Intervention process would the administrator check the file for incident reports or contracts?

4. Who gets a copy of the Incident Report?

5. If a student is returned to the office as the result of an inappropriate behavior, the minimum consequence is a behavior contract. What are the six major components of a behavior contract?

6. Who gets a copy of the behavior contract?

7. There may be a time when a student receives a consequence beyond a written contract when an Incident Report is in effect. What is an example of a behavior that warrants an adjustment in the penalty process?

8. Following the suggested penalty process, what is the penalty for a student sent to your office during the time a contract is in effect?

9. What is the consequence for a student sent to your office for arguing with a teacher? This is his fifth trip to the office this year, but no active contracts are in his file.

Answers
1. a) Call to parents and
   b) the Administrative Intervention process.
2. Potential future consequences and administrator's signature.
3. After the student is under gross control, as a part of the process of checking with the referring teacher, check the files for reports/contracts.
4. Only the administrator.
5. a) Name of student
   b) Inappropriate behavior
   c) Name of teacher
   d) The consequence for contract violation
   e) Date contract expires
   f) Signatures of student and administrator
6. Student, parents, teacher(s) and administrative file.
7. Answers vary; Examples including hitting a teacher, starting a fire, and threatening with a knife would be a few.
8. In-school suspension.
9. a) The Administrative Intervention process
   b) Call parents
   c) A new contract

In-School Suspension

In-School Suspension

In-school suspension is a term that connotes different meanings to different people. **In-school suspension is not designed to punish a student spontaneously, but rather to deliver a contractual penalty a student pays for having engaged in inappropriate behavior–usually on more than two occasions.**

In order to preserve student's rights, precautions are necessary in the administration the in-school suspension process. First and foremost the administration should consider such physical characteristics such as: the size of the room, ventilation, temperature, lighting, and other related factors. In addition, the length of time a student spends in peer isolation must be carefully monitored.

Students are not placed in in-school suspension until they are totally under instructional control. In-school suspension is viewed as the additional consequence (again, in addition to the phone call to the parents and the Administrative Intervention process itself) that will be administered as the result of an active contractual agreement. All of the cooling off and regaining self-control takes place in your office during the Crisis Stage and Intensive Teaching phase of the process. In-school suspension is a penalty to be paid, nothing more. As an administrator, you've lived up to your part of the contract; now the student must live up to his.

The in-school suspension room should meet all of the basic physical characteristics of comfort afforded to all students: clean, well-lit, well-ventilated, of adequate size, and safe (including appropriate exits). It should also include a good desk, and a good straight-back chair. The room must also be located so that it can be frequently monitored.

In-school suspension, like other consequences, takes place prior to the formulation of an apology. When the student meets the stipulations of in-school suspension, you will help him begin the classroom re-entry process with the formulation of an apology.

You must monitor carefully the amount of time a student is placed in in-school suspension. A minimum of a half-day may be very effective, but may also be a violation of the youth's rights because it might not take that much time to accomplish an assigned task. This is critical because there must be an assigned task. (Copying the first 50 words out of the dictionary or writing "I won't swear at my teacher" 500 times are violations of the student's rights and must not be used!)

One strategy for in-school suspension is the completion of a reasonable assignment, which would require a minimum of half a day to complete. Since this type of an assignment resembles homework, you want to be certain that the work assigned is on the student's independent work level (the student can do the work without teacher assistance). If the student is able to handle the assignment independently your assistance won't be required. Even if you have the time to offer instructional assistance, your assistance might be very reinforcing and the student isn't in in-school suspension to be reinforced. As a part of this in-school suspension assignment it can be helpful if you have an assortment of packets available for the student to work on. This enables you to give the student an assignment and not rely on a classroom teacher who not only may be busy, but also somewhat less than enthusiastic about providing the necessary independent work for a student sent to you with a behavior problem. However, many teachers have appropriate materials they are very willing to assign.

It is not as difficult as you may envision to produce a few packets that can be used by many students. Assignments may follow themes reinforcing the rationale for in-school suspension such as: 1) the formulation of a written apology to the teacher, 2) writing a theme on the value of following directions with the outlined points to be covered, 3) a written list of rationales for accepting criticism, following directions, accepting "no" for an answer, etc. Since inappropriate social skills are the cause of the suspensions and inappropriate social skills are one of the critical concerns of the school program, in-school suspension can be used appropriately to reinforce alternative appropriate social skill behaviors.

Many students are referred at mid-morning or mid-afternoon. When a student referred during this time has a contract that indicates in-school suspension is the appropriate penalty, you must determine the appropriate length of time to place the student in the suspension room. Generally it is preferable to complete the penalty by the end of that school day, but much is dependent upon the behavior that resulted in the referral and the behavior exhibited during the time the student is in the suspension room. The term of placement is a judgment call and in-school suspension—or the completion of the process—may be carried over to another day. However, when possible, try to conclude the process—the suspension, the preparation of the apology, and the delivery of the apology – by the end of the school day. This gives the student, the teachers, and you the opportunity to begin the next day on a positive note rather than a negative note.

Monitoring the student while in in-school suspension is extremely important. The student is expected to remain in a specific chair and work at the assigned task. Periodically, but at no less than 30-minute intervals, a monitor must check on the progress the student is making toward the completion of the assignment. As with all monitoring, the administrator must log the time of the monitoring and the status of the student. The student is placed in the suspension room for a period of time that is not to exceed a stated limitation (e.g., one-half day). The periodic check by the monitor may indicate that this student is doing exceptionally well (good social skills, on-task behavior, etc.) and should be released from suspension. This check also gives the student an opportunity to ask the monitor if he or she can get a drink of water or go to the bathroom. This is not to imply that the student should not have additional opportunities to request permission for either water or bathroom privileges. These privileges should be granted as requested, as long as appropriate social skill components are used in making the request. This is an excellent opportunity for the student to practice these skills and for you to reinforce their appropriate use.

When permission is granted for the student to go to the bathroom and/or get a drink of water, the student must always be accompanied by an adult. Since the student is not to engage in peer interaction during this period of suspension, the adult who is accompanying the student must be certain that the halls are cleared and the bathroom empty before allowing the student to proceed. The student is cautioned that any inappropriate behavior while in the suspension room, in the halls, or in the bathroom may lengthen the term of suspension.

The time the student spends in in-school suspension may include the lunch break. When this happens, be certain you provide the student with the appropriate amount of time and the regular meal served for lunch. You may elect to bring the lunch to the student so he is free from other student interaction. If the student is taken to the lunchroom, be careful to limit the interaction he has with peers or faculty members. Paying the penalty of in-school suspension should not be reinforced through peer or adult attention. Again, be careful not to deviate from the student's established lunch offerings. If the student eats in the school cafeteria, he is allowed the normal selections; if the student usually goes home for lunch, you may want to obtain parental permission for him to eat at school on this particular day. If the parents won't agree to having their child remain at school during the lunch period, send the student home and complete the suspension upon return. **Do not withhold lunch;** the penalty is in-school suspension, not deprivation of food. Students who don't go home for lunch but normally do leave the school campus during the lunch period should have the school cafeteria as the only option on this particular day. In the event the student is on medication, be certain that medication is taken on time in the prescribed dosage.

When used appropriately, in-school suspension is the best behavioral penalty available within the school setting. The use of in-school suspension allows you to keep the student in your building; while the student remains in your building, he remains under your control. He continues to have the opportunity to improve his social skills, but when a student is suspended out of school or is expelled from school, you lose control of the student and, as a result, you lose the teaching opportunities that may present themselves.

In-School Suspension

Process Summary

Students earn the penalty of in-school suspension through the behavior contract process. Placement in in-school suspension is a contractual agreement and becomes the consequence when you reach the consequence portion of the Teaching Interaction. The student must be well under control prior to this or any other consequence being administered—students are not sent to in-school suspension to cool off.

Students placed in in-school suspension must be given **meaningful** tasks to perform that will take a reasonable amount of time to complete. The student should be able to complete the tasks in less than one day, but not less than one-half day (with exceptions). If possible, the process should be completed during the day in which it was begun, including the appropriate apology to the teacher involved.

Students placed in in-school suspension will not be denied food, water, or bathroom privileges, but will be closely supervised during all activities that require them to be outside of the suspension room.

Students placed in in-school suspension must be monitored on a regular basis. They may be left alone for short periods of time, but an adult should be available to provide academic and social assistance when necessary.

The student neither prepares nor delivers the apology until the in-school suspension penalty has been completed.

In-School Suspension Process Review

1. In-school suspension can be used as a place for the student to gain control before you begin the Administrative Intervention process. **T - F?**

2. In-school suspension is usually a penalty that the student has signed off on as part of a behavior contract. **T - F?**

3. A student placed in in-school suspension is considered to be a potential runaway. **T - F?**

4. Give three examples of meaningful activities a student may engage in while in in-school suspension. _____

5. When a student needs to leave the suspension room, except in case of an emergency, such as a fire, he must be accompanied by a supervising adult. **T - F?**

6. When possible, the consequences, the apology, and the complete process are finalized before the end of the school day. **T - F?**

7. It is extremely important that a student placed in in-school suspension be monitored on a regular basis. **T - F?**

8. Which of the following is not a criterion for selection of an in-school suspension room? 1) the size of the room, 2) ventilation, 3) temperature, 4) lighting 5) a pop machine. _____

Answers
1. False. The student should be placed in in-school suspension only as part of the penalty.
2. True.
3. False. He is totally under instructional control prior to placement.
4. Answers vary. 1) classwork, 2) prepared packets, 3) formulation of apology, 4) listing rationales for appropriate behavior, etc.
5. True. No interaction with peers - accompanied for food, water, and bathroom privileges.
6. True. Begin the next day on a positive note.
7. True.
8. A pop machine.

Special Cases

Special Cases

The process does not infer that each time a student enters your office he will not be treated as a special case—**each student is special and should be treated as special.** You will find, however, that there will be incidents that involve multiple students, as well as several separate incidents that you will be bombarded with all at once. Let's sort out a few of them.

Fighting

When two or more students are referred to the office as a result of fighting, it will be important that you deal with them separately. Have the student who is under the best instructional control (a judgment call on your part) remain in an outer office, under supervision, while you work with the most involved student. Many administrators don't attempt to place blame for starting or being involved in a fight. The age-old adage, "it takes two to fight" is useful and both parties will be treated similarly with similar consequences.

There will be exceptions to this rule and there will certainly be times when one student is only protecting himself and has little if any recourse. Under such circumstances the consequences certainly will not be equal. However, keep in mind that both students could have exercised several options to avoid the fight. These options can be explored when you or the student is at the point of describing the appropriate behavior. The student has the option of telling someone else the situation is volatile and another student is pushing him toward a defensive action. The student often has the option of walking away from the situation. Your rationale: fighting is a situation that will not be tolerated on a job and both parties involved are in danger of being terminated.

When dealing with each student separately, follow all of the steps of Administrative Intervention, including the basic step of talking with the adult(s) who were involved.

At the conclusion of your intervention and after the administration of the consequences, each student will be required to deliver a minimum of two apologies—one to the adult(s) involved, even if the adult did nothing more than report the fight, and another to the other student involved in the incident (the students must ultimately apologize to each other). It should be noted, however, that the two (or more) students involved in the incident do not come together for any reason until all parties have practiced and are prepared to deliver an apology.

Fighting is, and should be, treated as a serious offense. If the fight took place in a classroom before a group of students, the students exhibiting the inappropriate behavior may also be required to apologize to the entire group prior to being readmitted.

Consequences for involvement in a fight vary from district to district and no attempt has been made to place them in degrees of acceptability. Many consequences involve school or board policy and the best that can be accomplished is to work within the policy. However, a great deal of teaching can take place before consequences are administered and, as with other incidents, the student(s) will learn a skill (how to disagree appropriately) that they will have an opportunity to use at some later date. Keep in mind also that a bad school or school board policy can be changed, and if you feel your policy is not in the best interest of the students, you can be the one to initiate the change. Often, as a result of policy, a student receives out-of-school suspension or expulsion. While these consequences may seem to be appropriate, you will want to remember that, under those conditions, the student is no longer under your direct control or supervision and his learning opportunities may be limited. Under normal circumstances you may want to consider in-school suspension as the most appropriate consequence for fighting.

Office Overload

There will be times when you are inundated by referrals to your office. The phases of the moon, changes in the weather, high tides, and many other unrelated phenomena have been viewed as the cause for inappropriate behavior resulting in a referral to your office. When more than one student is sent to your office at one time, or if you are in the midst of an intervention with a student and another student is referred to you, you must determine which student(s) is(are) under gross control and can maintain gross control while you deal with a more behaviorally involved student. You may have begun working with a student when you are presented with another student who is totally out of control. If that's the case, ask the student you have been working with to sit in your outer office, or at some other designated, supervised station. Usually the words, "John, you'll have to excuse me for a few minutes; I have to work with someone who needs me more than you do. I'd like to have you wait with my secretary and I'll be with you as soon as possible," will result in his maintaining gross control while you work with student #2. However, you may also determine that student #2 is the one under the best control and he should be the one who waits while you continue to work with student #1, again letting student #2 know that another student needs you more than he does. The process of needs determination and priority may continue to student #3, #4, #5, etc. You still work only with one student at a time while others are waiting elsewhere for your assistance.

In the event you continue to find yourself in impossible situations resulting from having to work with large numbers of students, it may become necessary that more than one person be designated to work with disruptive students. Consistency is important, and you will want to be certain an additional interventionist is really needed before someone else is added to the roster. Besides the potential problem with consistency, additional personnel, when they are not needed, can result in lack of regular involvement by the interventionists. There just may not be enough opportunities to work with disruptive students and skills may become dull or forgotten.

To stay sharp, an interventionist should have the opportunity to work with a minimum of three to five students per week, however, if you find you are working with more than four or five per day, you may need assistance. Just don't be too hasty in adding personnel; when the program is first initiated the students may not be familiar with the teaching processes and your lower tolerances may cause a time involvement the students will later help you resolve.

Drug Involvement/Alcohol Involvement

Even under the best circumstances, sooner or later a student will be referred to your office who is obviously "under the influence." **The Administrative Intervention process is of little value in dealing with a student even mildly under the influence.** This student should not be worked with until all signs of chemical involvement have dissipated–usually the next day. Until you can work with the student regarding the problem, you may refer the student home, to authorities, or whatever school policy dictates. The point is, you cannot use the techniques of Administrative Intervention until the person is sober and responsible for his behavior. However, if your policy does allow school re-entry, you will want to use all of the Administrative Intervention techniques before the student is re-admitted to the school program.

Rules to Remember in Using Administrative Intervention

Rule One - Separate the student from his behavior. In your own mind be able to separate the student from the behaviors he is or is not exhibiting.

Remember, you are dealing with a student (person) you like who is presently acting or has acted in a way that is not acceptable in your school program. Don't be manipulated by statements like "You're just like that teacher–you don't like me either." It's not a matter of personal like or dislike–that's not the issue! Your willingness to deal only with the inappropriate behavior, as well as your own verbal and nonverbal behavior, leaves no doubt in the student's mind that you really do like him, but you owe it to him as a friend, and it's your professional obligation to teach him appropriate, useful behaviors. Keep in mind when these inappropriate behaviors occur outside of school, they can cost him his job! Your job is to prepare him to become a responsible citizen in society.

Rule Two - Remain rational.

No matter how irrational, upset, uncooperative, and verbally abusive the student may be in your office, it is critical that you model rational and controlled behavior. There is nothing less effective in working with an irrational person than having another irrational person as an interventionist. It is important for students to observe that being able to yell, threaten, or in any other way behave in an abrasive manner, is not a privilege reserved for adults. If you lose control and yell and swear, the student may generalize that all he has to do is wait a few years and then he can behave that way towards others.

Rational behavior on the part of the adult, however, can only come about if that person knows what he is doing and has a set process to follow. Difficult children can engage in behavior that is frustrating to many adults. Frustration can easily lead to irrational behavior, which results in either the student escalating his or her inappropriate and irrational behavior or the adult doing or saying something that may be relationship-damaging and later regretted.

Rational behavior on your part includes maintaining a calm voice tone, using the student's first name, using empathy statements, avoiding judgmental terms by describing behavior specifically, verbally praising appropriate student behavior, and even asking for someone to replace you if and when you find yourself becoming frustrated.

Rule Three - Don't rush the process.

Even though you have a million things to do each and every day, you can't afford to short-change your students. They deserve the best and you can provide it! The steps outlined in this book are designed to be used to maximize the process' effectiveness. Just as you don't expect students to learn to read or to master the multiplication tables in one day, you cannot expect students to learn or to be able to use appropriate social skills consistently in just a few minutes. The Administrative Intervention procedures may take a couple of hours to complete. The minimum time, however, is generally no less than 20 minutes even with the most cooperative student. There are many opportunities to take breaks and then come back to the student later to continue the process. Take advantage of these breaks if you need them. The student's future school career is, at this moment, dependent more upon you and your skills than upon whether he misses Tuesday's social studies or math class.

Rule Four - Don't expect students to learn everything in one sitting.

Students sent to your office because of disruptive behavior have often been practicing those inappropriate social behaviors for many years. As with Rule Three, you do not expect that learning social skills will take place any more rapidly than learning certain academic skills. One trip to your office does not assure that the need for teaching social skills is eliminated forever. Many students need repeated instruction, consistent consequences and, above all, a caring instructor (administrator) who is willing to assist the student in the learning process.

Rule Five - Don't fear or avoid crisis situations.

Remember, you are in a position of authority; act like it. Your students and your staff deserve strong and effective leadership; avoiding crisis situations places the responsibility on someone else's shoulders. Dealing with disruptive students in the manner prescribed does nothing but enhance your image with staff and students!

Rule Six - View the crisis situation as a teaching opportunity for yourself.

As a school administrator you don't often get the chance to teach and instruct the students. It is also a fact that others don't realize that you got your position not because you were a poor teacher, but because you were effective with kids. You have a lot to offer in terms of teaching social skills to the students who need them the most—the students sent out of their classrooms to your office. But you must be careful not to counsel or in any other way avoid directly instructing the student in the use of those skills he needs to return to and function effectively in the classroom. The student's social errors must be viewed no differently than an error in math or in punctuation. They are all opportunities to learn, and opportunities for you to teach.

Bibliography

Bauer, G.L. (1985). Restoring order to the public school. *Phi Delta Kappan*, 66, 488-491.

Brown, L.J., Black, D.D., & Downs, J.C. (1984). *School Social Skills Manual.* New York, NY: Slosson Educational Publications, Inc.

Bryan, T. (1982). Social skills of learning disabled children and youth: An overview. *Learning Disability Quarterly*, 5, 332-333.

Carroll, T.L. & Elliott, S.N. (1984). Social Competence and social skills: Development, assessment and intervention. *School Psychology Review*, 13, 265.

Cartledge, G. & Milburn, J.F. (1978). The case for teaching social skills in the classroom: A review. *Review of Educational Research*, 48, 133-156.

Daly, D. & Daly, P. (1977). *Trainee Manual for Pre-Service Workshop in the Boys Town Teaching Family Model.* Boys Town, NE: Father Flanagan's Boys' Home.

Downs, J.C., Kutsick, K., & Black, D.D. (1985). The teaching interaction: A systematic approach to developing social skills in disruptive (and non-disruptive) students. *Techniques*, 1, 304-310.

Gallup, G.H. (1987). The 19th annual gallup poll of the public's attitudes toward the public schools. *Phi Delta Kappan*, 69, 17-30.

Gresham, F.M. (1984). Social skills and self-efficiency for exceptional children. *Exceptional Children*, 51, 253-261.

Hops, H. & Cobb, J.A. (1973). Survival behaviors in the educational setting: Their implications for research and intervention. In L.A. Hammerlynk, L.C. Handy, and E.J. Mash (Eds.), *Behavior Change.* Champaign, IL: Research Press, 193-208.

Justiz, M.J. (1984). It's time to make every minute count. *Phi Delta Kappan*, 65, 483-485.

Kain, C.J., Downs, J.C., & Black, D.D. (1988). Social skills in the school curriculum: A systematic approach. *NASSP Bulletin*, 72, 107-110.

Bibliography

Phillips, E.L., Phillips, E.A., Fixsen, D.L., & Wolf, M.M. (1974). *The Teaching Family Handbook* (rev. ed.). Lawrence, KS: University of Kansas Printing Service.

Squires, D.A., Huitt, W.G., & Segars, J.K. (1984). *Effective Schools and Classrooms: A Research-Based Perspective.* Alexandria, VA: Association for Supervision and Curriculum Development.

Stephens, T.M. (1978). *Social Skills in the Classroom.* Columbus, OH: Cedars Press, Inc.